Cookery for Working-Men's Wives

by

Francis Henry Underwood

APPLEWOOD BOOKS
Bedford, Massachusetts

Cookery for Working-Men's Wives

was originally published in

1890

ISBN: 978-1-4290-1223-2

Thank you for purchasing an Applewood book. Applewood reprints America's lively classics— books from the past that are still of interest to the modern reader.
For a free copy of
a catalog of our
bestselling
books,
write
to us at:
Applewood Books
Box 365
Bedford, MA 01730
or visit us on the web at:
For cookbooks: foodsville.com
For our complete catalog: awb.com

Prepared for publishing by HP

The Helping Hand Club

Issue No. 1

COOKERY

FOR

WORKING-MEN'S WIVES

REPRINTED FROM
Reports from the Consuls of the United States,
No. 107.

NEW ALMADEN

1890

COOKERY

FOR

WORKING-MEN'S WIVES.

REPORT BY UNITED STATES CONSUL UNDERWOOD, OF GLASGOW.

I have the honor to state that I was lately invited to be present at a "demonstration" of a school for women in cooking and other branches of domestic economy. I should not, perhaps, be justified in making this report if the instruction followed ordinary lines. The novelty consists partly in cheapness, and having seen a good, palatable, and nutritious meal for six persons prepared at a cost of 1s. (24 cents), and having observed the ameliorating influences flowing out from the school, I have thought some account of it might be of use in certain crowded districts of the United States, where the advice and assistance of the benevolent is needed.

The school was established three years ago in Govan, a large ship-building town adjoining Glasgow, by Mrs. John Elder, widow of the well-known ship-builder, and all the expenses thus far have been paid by her. It is held in Broomloan Hall, belonging to the Established Presbyterian Church, under the charge of Rev. Dr. Macleod, who, with Mrs. Macleod, has taken an active part in promoting the work.

The teacher, Miss Martha H. Gordon, is a sensible and practical woman, and has shown great tact in gaining the good-will and sympathy of those among whom she has labored. This confidence appears to be an indispensable prerequisite; the distrustful attitude of those needing help often frustrates any attempt to benefit them.

The school, though primarily aiming at humble things, seems likely to have the broader effect of raising the plane of life and morals.

The pupils are in two classes (1), mothers and unmarried women over twenty, and (2) girls of twenty and under. Girls are not generally received until they have left school. Each class meets twice a week for lessons in cooking and once a week for darning and mending. Instruction is also given in starching and ironing.

In the leisure hours of every day Miss Gordon goes, as a friendly adviser, to houses in the district, wherever she is asked—sometimes to pupils' houses, sometimes to others—giving practical instructions upon all household matters. The mothers' class this last season numbered over two hundred, the younger class about one hundred and thirty. The attendance was naturally more regular in the latter. The numbers in both classes have been far too large for one teacher. From seventy-five to one hundred should be the maximum number, and for the next season additional teachers will be employed.

The two classes represent about two hundred families, all of which, and a great many more, have been often visited by the teacher. The pupils are the wives and daughters of workmen in ship-yards and machine-shops, and of common laborers. The teacher thinks there is a visible improvement in the condition of at least thirty families, with hopeful signs in more. The gain is in personal neatness, in manners, speech, and general tone. The houses are more tidy and the children better clothed, and there are other cheerful signs, such as flower-pots in the windows. The teacher thinks the younger pupils will be lifted permanently, and not relapse when they become mothers of families. At present the chief obstacle in the way of improvement is the want of education. The girls read fairly, but write with difficulty.

The heads of these families earn from 15s. to 25s. per week ($3.75 to $6.25). For a "house" of one room (meaning one room in an apartment house) the rent is from £6 to £7 per annum ($29.16 to $34.02); for a house of two rooms from £7 to £9 ($34.02 to $43.74). The taxes, water, and gas amount to about one-fifth as much as the rent in addition. A very little arithmetic is necessary to show how small a sum is left for clothing and food. From these statements the importance of a system of instruction by which food can be prepared at a low cost will be evident.

In many respects the instruction has been general—that is, as to the ways and means by which all successful cooking is best carried on; but the materials have been chosen with rigid economy, so as to produce satisfactory results with the least money. It is easy enough to cook good dinners when there is an unlimited larder.

Mrs. Elder offered a series of prizes in money and in books, from £2 ($9.72) downwards, and on the day of the "demonstration" there was a long show of bowls filled with hotch-potch (a broth with an abundance of minced vegetables), of oat-cake, and of "scones" (thin wheaten cakes, made light with baking-powder). There were shown, also, specimens of mending clothes, of darning stockings, of ironing shirts, etc. The teacher, assisted by two pupils, stood upon a platform before the cooking range, and went through all the operations required to prepare and cook a meal. Every process and mode of manipulation was explained step by step. This occupied nearly two hours, and there were produced several excellent dishes; a fish soup, a kidney and liver soup, and a meat pie were the most successful. The fish soup was made of a large cod's head, with the addition of rice, onions, and potatoes. The kettle contained over 6 quarts, and the cost was a little more than sixpence. The meat pie is called "sea pie," because it is in general use among sailors. The peculiar excellence of Miss Gordon's method is in making the meat tender and the crust light and not greasy. The flavor was excellent. The exact cost of each dish was given.

The competition was not for the production of any one dish. Each competitor furnished in writing a plan for a series of fourteen dinners for a family of six, no dinner to exceed 1s. (24 cents) in cost, the price and quantity of each ingredient to be stated. One dinner was produced by each, for which the soup was broth. Each competitor also baked scones and oat-cakes.

After the examination of the specimens of cookery, mending, etc., the company adjourned to the large hall. The chair was taken by Dr. McLean, surgeon-general of the British army, who made a speech full of good sense and of practical knowledge, and with a clearness and beauty of phrase that left nothing to be desired. The hall was completely filled by the pupils and their families and friends. The prizes were given to the successful competitors, and a large number of books were bestowed upon other meritorious pupils. The scene was really affecting, mainly on account of the condition of the people interested. The bestowal of honors at a university was a commonplace affair in comparison.

The time will soon come, if it has not come already, when

efforts of the kind here described will be needed in the more populous districts of the United States, and without depreciating the benevolent institutions which aim to diffuse intellectual and moral influences among the working people, I submit that showing them how to live comfortably upon their small wages and inducing them to cultivate habits of order, neatness, and self-respect is not less important.

F. H. UNDERWOOD,
Consul.

UNITED STATES CONSULATE,
Glasgow, September 6, 1888.

[Inclosure in Consul Underwood's report.]

COOKERY FOR WORKING-MEN'S WIVES.

(By Martha H. Gordon, as taught in Mrs. John Elder's domestic cookery classes, at Govan, near Glasgow, Scotland.)

PREFACE.

One of the principal objects of the instruction in domestic economy provided and organized in Govan some years ago by Mrs. John Elder, is to teach plain and economical cookery to women in classes, and especially at their homes.

Since this movement was begun, domestic economy has been more largely taken up by school-boards in classes from the fifth standard upwards. Obviously, however, great need still exists, and must continue to exist—many children leaving the schools before they reach the fifth standard—for instruction of the kind, and given in the mode contemplated by Mrs. Elder. The recipes in this little cookery book are among those which I have been in the habit of teaching and illustrating, in fulfillment of the duties assigned to me by Mrs. Elder. They are here printed in the hope that they may be useful, not only to those attending the classes here and in the homes of Govan, but to the wives and daughters of artisans elsewhere. Some recipes for more advanced cookery have been added, together with directions in regard to washing, sanitary hints, etc. But it will be observed that the great aim kept in view is to help working-men's wives to provide thoroughly good and nutritrious food for their families at the smallest possible cost.

Some of the ingredients are, perhaps, not commonly used, but the use of them does not involve much trouble, and they will be found to make nutritious and substantial meals.

(1) Let me say, do not despise the importance of proper food to the human body. In order to nourish properly every part of the human body food should be carefully prepared and often varied. It is one of the duties of women, and a very important one, to attend to this. The mother of a family should grudge no trouble to gain skill and knowledge as to the best method of providing nourishing and palatable food for her husband and children. My experience has shown me that there are very many good, nutritious

dishes to be made at exceedingly small cost. Unhappily, there are comparatively few who will take enough thought or trouble to prepare them. How many homes would be healthier, brighter, and happier if our women could only be brought to see how much depends on them, and bestir themselves in the matter.

(2) Do not despise the use of what are called scraps of meat. Scraps of meat, which can be got cheap from the butcher, will, with care and attention, make good pies and stews, and are as nutritious as more expensive cuts. A working-man's wife who studies economy and tries by careful cooking to get all the nourishment possible out of food will be able to feed her family on a tenth of what one who is careless and ignorant requires.

(3) The great art in cooking is to keep in all the nutrition, salts, etc., of our foods, and to prevent them from being wasted in vapor up the chimney or through the house. All foods, whether heat-giving, flesh-forming, or stimulant, should therefore be cooked so as to keep in their several juices and flavors. All foods over or under done are wasteful.

(4) Of the various modes of cooking I think one of the most economical, if attended to, is stewing. A clean pot with a close lid is required for stewing. After the stew is in the pot and warm do not remove the lid till it is ready, but give the pot a shake once or twice to keep it from sticking, and when done you will have a dish with all the nourishment and flavor in it.

(5) To boil meat for soup put it in cold water, to dissolve all the juices. To boil meat so as to keep in the juices put it in boiling water and boil fast for ten minutes, to form a crust to keep in the juices, then simmer.

(6) All bones for soup should be boiled for some hours, when the fire is not otherwise in use, so as to take all the goodness out of them, and this has not been done until they are perfectly light. The common practice of taking only two hours to boil a bone for soup is both careless and extravagant. If you wish to make a penny go as far as possible by preventing the loss from any article of food you cook of a single element of flavor or nutritiveness, which is the object of perfect and economical cookery, remember to boil long and slowly, keeping the lid of your pot on as much as possible. By this means a pot of soup costing only a few pennies will be more savory and enjoyable than one costing many shillings and carelessly made.

(7) Some sweet herbs, such as thyme, marjoram, mint, etc. (which can be grown at your windows), or a little celery seeds and two or

three cloves tied in a bit of muslin are a great improvement to many soups and stews.

(8) It is much better, when you can, to grate your vegetables; both the flavor and color is better than when boiled and put through a sieve.

(9) In selecting vegetables see that they are perfectly fresh. After washing and trimming them, leave them in cold water and salt for an hour, so as to get rid of any slugs and make them crisp if drooping. To cook green vegetables, such as cabbage, greens, etc., have plenty of water with salt and a little soda in it, and when quite boiling put in the vegetables and boil quickly. Do not close lid of pot, and remove all scum as it rises. Without attention to these directions the vegetables will not be a good color. All water that green vegetables have been boiled in should be taken to the ash pit, as if put down the sink the smell would be very unpleasant in the house. With roots, such as turnips, carrots, etc., the lid may be kept on the pot. Turnips should be peeled rather thickly, then cut in four, or in slices, and boiled till tender. Carrots are only scraped, not peeled, then cut lengthways in four, and boiled till tender. If onions be boiled whole, care must be taken not to cut their tops too short, as they will fall to pieces. Never leave vegetables in the water after they are cooked enough.

(10) The following recipes are specially intended for the ordinary kitchen utensils and open fires. Some of them may appear to be repetitions, but this is not the case, as the same ingredients, when cooked in a different way, will produce a different result. Should any of the recipes seem long, it must be remembered that they, in some cases, give complete dinners, and so contain several recipes in one.

(11) The quantities specified are, as a rule, given in proportion suitable for a family from four to six in number, and the prices given are averages. M. H. GORDON.

PLAIN HOUSEHOLD COOKERY.

Porridge.—To make really good porridge let the water come to the boiling point before the meal is put in. Pour the meal in from the left hand in a continuous stream, stirring all the time till it comes to the boil. In this consists the chief art of porridge making, and on its being well done depends the smoothness. Allow it to boil for ten minutes, then add the salt. Salt has a tendency to harden, and would prevent the meal from swelling. Boil for ten minutes after the salt has been added. Dish and take with milk.

The quantity and consistency of the porridge must be regulated by the cook.

Wheat meal porridge.—Have 1 quart of water at the boiling point; take three good handfuls, or about 2½ teacupfuls, of wheat meal; pour the meal regularly from the left hand, stirring all the time. There must be no lumps in it. Boil for ten minutes, add salt to taste, and boil for ten minutes more. Serve with milk, treacle, or stewed fruit.

Porridge (for indigestion).—One pound barley meal, 1 pound oatmeal, 2 pounds wheat meal, 1 pound Indian meal; mix well together, proceed in the same way as with wheat meal porridge, but boil for half an hour instead of twenty minutes.

To make a good cup of tea.—One teaspoonful of tea to every half-pint of water; have the teapot well rinsed in hot water; put in the tea, take a piece of paper and close the spout, set the teapot near the fire, but not so near as to burn, for ten minutes; have the water boiling and add; do not let it stand longer than six minutes after adding the water. Remove the paper from the spout and you will find you have a cup of tea with all the aroma in it. Sugar and cream to taste.

Be sure not to allow the water to boil too long. It is best taken when it first comes through the boil.

Coffee.—One teaspoonful of coffee to each breakfast cup. An earthenware pot is best; have it very clean and hot. Put in the coffee, close the spout to keep in all the aroma, let it stand at the fire, not too near, for ten minutes; when the water boils, put it into the pot and cover close. Do not boil your coffee, but see that your lid is very close, so that all the fine flavor is preserved.

How to boil eggs.—Put 1 pint of water in a small pan; let it boil; put in the egg; if small, three minutes will set it; if large, four minutes. When boiling several eggs see that they are as nearly as possible the same size. Ten minutes is required to boil an egg hard.

Poached eggs.—Put 1 pint of water in a small pan, with half a teaspoonful of salt, and a tablespoonful of vinegar; let it boil; break the egg carefully into the pan, and simmer for four minutes. Take it out carefully and serve on toast.

French toast.—Break and beat an egg well, add a pinch of salt and one gill of milk, dip some neat slices of bread in on both sides. Have your frying-pan with some hot dripping ready, then fry the bread a light brown.

This is good with stewed rhubarb laid on the top.

A nice breakfast.—One-fourth pound of old cheese, a teacupful of milk, two eggs, a pinch of salt, a pinch of pepper, a small bit of butter. Cut the cheese very thin, put it into a frying-pan with half of the milk, butter, pepper and salt. Stir until the cheese is melted, then add the eggs, well beaten, with the rest of the milk. Cook for one minute and spread on hot toast.

Eggs stewed with cheese.—One egg for each person. Let them set in a frying-pan, remove them to a plate. Cut some cheese very thin; put it on the top of the eggs, with salt and pepper to taste. Set before the fire or in the oven to swell, and serve hot.

Ham and eggs.—Put your sliced ham on in a cold frying-pan, turn it two or three times, taking care not to let it burn. When sufficiently done lay the ham on a nice hot plate. Break the eggs into a cup, taking care not to break the yolks; slip one at a time into the frying-pan and baste with the ham fat. Keep the eggs as round as possible, lift with a slice, and lay on the ham.

Omelet (plain).—In making an omelet care should be taken to have the pan quite hot and perfectly dry. Put into the frying-pan 1 ounce of lard, beat very gently (the lard must not get brown). The eggs are to be very lightly beaten, only long enough to mix them and no more. Break 4 eggs into a basin, half a teaspoonful of salt, and a quarter of a teaspoonful of pepper; mix, pour into a hot pan, and keep mixing quickly, till they are delicately set. Turn in the edges, let it rest a moment to set, turn it over on a dish, and serve.

Omelet.—Two eggs, 1 teacupful of milk, 1 tablespoonful of corn flour, 1 tablespoonful sugar, pinch of salt, teaspoonful essence vanilla. Put the yolks of the eggs in a basin and stir them till they are light. Add the milk to them, then add, gradually, to the corn flour and other ingredients in another basin; stir till very smooth; beat the white of the eggs to a snow and add them very gently with the essence vanilla to the rest of the mixture. Have a hot frying-pan, put in a little lard and melt, pour in all the mixture, and hold it over a gentle fire for a quarter of an hour, till set and well risen; brown the sap before the fire, or bake for a quarter of an hour in the oven.

Colored eggs for Easter.—Eggs can be dyed a pretty color with the juice of a beet root, or the peel of onions boiled in the water; or, if you have a patch of fancy print, bind it round the egg and boil it, and it will leave the impression. Wash the eggs clean before boiling. Easter eggs should be boiled for ten minutes.

Kedgeree.—One pound fish, one-fourth pound rice, 3 eggs, 1 ounce butter. Wash rice well, put on in boiling water, and boil till soft; boil the fish and take away all bones and skin and separate into flakes. Boil 3 eggs for ten minutes, then throw into cold water to prevent their turning black, then peel and cut fine. Drain all the water from the rice, put it on the fire to dry, add the butter, salt, pepper, fish and eggs (saving one of the yolks), let it all warm, then dish and grate the yolk of the egg over it.

Pea soup and potatoes.—One pound split peas, $1\frac{1}{2}d.$; vegetables, $1\frac{1}{2}d.$; one-fourth stone* potatoes, $1\frac{1}{2}d.$; total, $4\frac{1}{2}d.$

Wash the peas, and leave them soak over night; put them on with 1 gallon of the water in which they were soaked, and the onions cut fine; boil for one hour and a half, add carrot and turnip and two potatoes, all grated; boil for another half hour, then add a teaspoonful of powdered mint, and serve hot. To be taken with potatoes.

Barley broth.—One pound mutton or beef bones, $1d.$; one-half pound barley, $1d.$; one-half pound of peas, $1d.$; cabbage, turnip, carrot, parsnip, leeks, parsley, and celery, $1d.$; total, $4d.$ In most places an assorted lot of vegetables can be got for $1d.$ or $2d.$, according to quantity.

Nothing can be more nourishing or wholesome than broth. It

---
* NOTE.—The stone equals 14 pounds avoirdupois.

is advisable to make sufficient for two days, as many think the second day's broth warmed up is the best. It can be made of beef or mutton. The neck of mutton makes very sweet broth, but some prefer a cut of boiling beef with marrow. Be sure to have a pot with a good fitting lid. Put on the meat with 2 gallons of water, barley, and peas (if peas are used, they must be soaked the night before), and boil for one hour, then add the cabbage, turnip, carrot, and parsnip, cut small, and part of the carrot grated. Boil very slowly with lid closed for half an hour, then add leeks, parsley, and celery; boil for another half-hour; in all, boil for two hours, and serve.

Sheep's head broth.—Head and trotters, 6d; barley and peas, 1d.; mixed vegetables, 1½d.; total, 8½d.

Get head and trotters singed; have the head split, take out the brains, wash every part well; pierce the eyes, and wash the skin well with the liquor that flows out; scape out the eye cavities with a knife, then put the head and trotters in a pail of clean water, with a little salt and soda; let them steep all night; take them out, and scrape them well; put them in the pot with 1 gallon of water, a teacupful of peas, and three-fourths of a teacupful of barley, boil for three-quarters of an hour; add half a turnip cut in slices, the other half with carrot, parsnip, and cabbage cut very small; add leeks, celery, parsley cut small, and boil for another hour; dish the broth, and serve head and trotters with the slices of turnip for garnish. Sheep's head broth requires longer boiling than other broths.

Fish soup.—Cod head, 1d.; vegetables (carrot, onion and parsley), 1½d.; one-half pound rice, 0½d.; one-half stone potatoes, 2d.; total, 5d.

Get a large cod head, wash it well; put in on with cold water (1 gallon), and boil for an hour, then put it through a sieve or clean coarse cloth; wash the rice well and add; cut the onions very fine, and add; grate the carrot, and boil very slowly with lid closed for one hour; then add chopped parsley and all the fish taken from the head, with pepper and salt to taste. Serve hot with potatoes. A little milk will improve the soup. It is very like oyster soup.

Mock kidney soup and potatoes.—Two pounds of liver, 6d.; vegetables (carrot, turnip, onion), 1d.; one-half stone potatoes, 3d.; total, 10d.

Put on half of the liver with 1 gallon of water; boil very slowly for an hour, then take it out, and grate it; have the other half cut in nice, small pieces, and add ; grate the carrot and turnip, and one potato, but do not add the potato until fifteen minutes before you take the soup off the fire; cut the onion very fine, and add it with the liver, carrot and turnip; boil very slowly for one and one-half hours with lid close. Pepper and salt to taste, and serve hot with potatoes.

Potato soup and fried beans.—One-fourth stone potatoes, 1½d.; bone, 1d.; vegetables, 1d.; 1 pound haricot beans, 1½d.; 2 ounces dripping, 0¾d.; onions, 0¼d.; total, 6d.

Boil the bone for six hours in 1 gallon of water; cut the potatoes in six, and add; cut leeks fine, grate carrot and turnip, and add; boil for an hour with lid very close, then add a little parsley cut fine; pepper and salt to taste. Serve hot.

Beans: Soak the beans for sixteen hours, then boil them for two and one-half hours; drain them; have a hot pan ready, put in dripping, with onion cut fine, then add beans, and fry till of a pale, golden brown.

Rice soup and baked haricot beans.—One-half pound rice, 0¾d.; bone, 1d.; vegetables, 1d.; 1 pound beans, 1½d.; onions, 0½d.; 2 ounces dripping, 0¾d.; salt and pepper to taste; total, 5½d.

Soup: Boil the bone for six hours. When you are going to make your soup see that you have a gallon of the water that the bone was boiled in; add the rice, carrot and turnip, grated, leek cut up small, and a little parsley cut fine; boil for one hour; pepper and salt to taste.

Beans: Soak the beans over night; put them and the onions cut fine into a dish ; salt and pepper to taste; add dripping and a pint of water; cover with a close fitting lid, and bake in a slow oven for six hours. A most nutritious and savory dinner.

Rice soup, tripe and potatoes.—Sheep's bag, 2½d.; one-half pound rice, 0¾d.; vegetables, 1d.; one-fourth stone potatoes, 1½d.; total, 5¾d.

Clean the tripe well, and boil it slowly for five hours; take it out, and cut it up into small pieces, and put it into another saucepan with a pint of stock, keep lid close; let it simmer for two hours; to remainder of stock add water to make 1 gallon, add rice, and let it boil for half an hour slowly; cut leeks and parsley fine, grate carrot, and add; boil for another half-hour, and serve hot, with salt and pepper to taste. Serve tripe with potatoes.

Haricot bean soup and potatoes.—One-fourth stone potatoes, 1½d.; 1 pound beans, 1½d.; vegetables, 1d.; onions, 0½d.; one-fourth stone potatoes, 1½d.; total, 6d.

Wash the beans, and leave them to soak for sixteen hours. Put into a clean pot with a gallon of water and the onion cut fine. Boil very carefully and slowly for two hours, then add carrot, turnip and two potatoes, all grated, and boil for half an hour. Just before serving add a teaspoonful of powdered sage; salt and pepper to taste. Serve hot. To be taken with potatoes.

Mulligatawny soup.—A calf's head and feet, 4*d.*; pepper, salt, carrot and turnip, 1*d.*; apple, 1*d.*; onion, marjoram, thyme, curry powder and sugar, 1*d.*; total, 7*d.*

Scald the head and feet in hot water, having about the size of a nut of soda in the water; then scrape the hair all off, wash clean, and boil for about two hours; then strain the stock through a sieve or cloth; take all the meat from the bones, cut into small dice, and put it back into the soup; add water until you have 1 gallon; then cut the apple, onion, and half of the carrot and turnip into small dice, and fry them in a pan; grate the other half of the turnip and carrot, and add all to the soup, also a teaspoonful of powdered marjoram, curry powder, thyme, and sugar, pepper and salt to taste, and boil for one hour.

Mock cock-a-leekie (very good).—Two pounds veal, 6*d.*; leeks, 2*d.*; four cloves, blade of mace, one-half teaspoonful of celery seed, 1*d.*; total, 9*d.*

Boil the veal slowly for two hours in 1 gallon of water, with the cloves, mace and celery seed tied up in a muslin bag. When the veal has boiled two hours take it out and add the leeks, well washed and cut fine. Cut up the veal in small pieces, add to soup. When the leeks have boiled half an hour add the potato, grated; boil for fifteen minutes; take out the muslin bag. Salt and pepper to taste; serve hot.

Mock turtle soup.—Calf's head, a small piece of the lights, 6*d.*; small piece of the liver, one-fourth pound fat pork, 2*d.*; 1 teaspoonful of cinnamon, 1 of allspice, one-half of cloves, one-half of cayenne pepper, 1*d.*; 1 lemon, 1*d.*; one-half pound flour, 0½*d.*; 3 potatoes, 0½*d.*; 3 eggs, 3*d.*; total, 1*s.* 2*d.*

Wash and soak the head, lights, and liver for some hours. Boil them very carefully, keeping the lid close. Cut the meat up into small strips, fry the pork, cut it up into small pieces and add all to the soup. Veal should have 1 gallon. When it boils put in the cinnamon, allspice, cloves and cayenne pepper. Grate the rind of the lemon, add it with the juice to the soup. Grate the three potatoes and add. Brown the flour before the fire, mix it smooth, and add; let it all boil for ten minutes. Have 3 hard-boiled eggs, slice them up into the tureen, and pour the soup on the top of them. This recipe is equal to real turtle soup. It can be made with force meat balls, which are an improvement.

Sea pie and potatoes.—One pound scrap meat, 5d.; vegetables, 1d.; suet, 1d.; flour, 1d.; baking powder; one-fourth stone potatoes, 1½d.; total, 9½d.

Get nice fresh meat and cut it into small pieces. Wash and cut up onions, carrot, turnip; put into stew-pan with two cups of boiling water; set on the fire. Mince suet fine and mix with the flour, a pinch of salt, one-half teaspoonful of baking powder, mix with cold water, roll out paste the size of the pan lid, put it on top of the meat and vegetables, and let all steam for one and one-half hours at the side of the fire, not boiling but at the boil. When done cut the paste in four and take it out with the fork, then the meat and vegetables, and put the paste on top of all as it was in the pot. Serve hot with potatoes.

Potatoes and stewed tripe.—Sheep's bag, 2½d.; one-fourth stone potatoes, 1½d.; one-half pound onions, 0½d.; total, 4½d.

Get a sheep's bag and clean it well with hot water, not boiling but very hot, then leave it over night in salt and water, put it on and let it stew very gently for three hours in 2 pints of water. Cut up the onion very small, and cut the tripe up into nice pieces; return the tripe to the soup with onion and a large tablespoonful of flour, then stew for another hour. If you can afford it, 1d. worth of milk added to this would make it better. Serve hot with potatoes.

"Hot pot," or stewed mutton and potatoes.—One pound flank of mutton, 4½d.; carrot, turnip, onion, 1d.; one-fourth stone potatoes, 1½d.; total, 7d.

Wash and pare potatoes, cut into four or six; pare turnip, cut in slices; scrape carrot and cut in slices; cut onion fine; cut mutton into small pieces; put a little of it into the bottom of the stew-pan, then potatoes, onion, carrot, turnip, mixed with pepper and salt, then some more mutton, till all is in; add 1 pint of water, and steam for two hours. Serve hot.

German pie.—One-fourth stone potatoes, 1½d.; red herring, 0¾d.; 1 pound flour, 1½d.; one-fourth pound dripping, 1½d.; pepper, salt, baking powder, 0¼d.; total, 5½d.

Wash, pare and slice potatoes, soak the herring in warm water, and divide into flakes; put the sliced potatoes and herring into a pie dish, well mixed with a little pepper and 1 ounce of dripping. If the herring is not salt, add a little salt, cover, and bake for two hours.

Cover: Mix the flour and 3 ounces of dripping with a teaspoonful of baking powder and a saltspoonful of salt; make a stiff paste with cold water, roll out to the size of the pie dish and cover. Serve hot.

A good "poor man's" pie.—One-fourth stone potatoes, $1\frac{1}{2}d.$; 3 ounces tapioca, $0\frac{1}{2}d.$; one-half pound onions, $0\frac{1}{2}d.$; 1 pound flour, $1\frac{1}{2}d.$; one-fourth pound dripping, $1\frac{1}{2}d.$; pepper, salt, baking powder, $0\frac{1}{4}d.$: total, $5\frac{3}{4}d.$

Mode: Wash, pare and slice the potatoes. Have the tapioca washed and soaked in cold water for an hour before it is wanted. Cut onion fine. Take 1 ounce of the dripping and put a little in the bottom of a pie dish, then onion, then some of the soaked tapioca, then potatoes, salt and pepper. Repeat till all are in, then cover. Take the 1 pound of flour, 3 ounces dripping, a teaspoonful of baking powder and a saltspoonful of salt, mix well and add cold water to make a stiff paste, roll out and cover. Bake for two hours. Serve hot.

A good savory pie.—One pound ox liver, $3d.$; one-fourth stone potatoes, $1\frac{1}{2}d.$; 1 pound flour, $1\frac{1}{2}d.$; one-fourth pound lard, $1\frac{1}{4}d.$; pepper, salt, onion and baking powder, $0\frac{3}{4}d.$; total, $8d.$

Mode: Cut the liver in small pieces, also the onion. Pare the potatoes very thin, cut in slices, and put them in pie dish in layers with pepper and salt. When all in, add water till three parts full.

Cover: Take flour, lard, a teaspoonful of baking powder, and a saltspoonful of salt; mix well; add cold water to make a paste; roll out and cover pie dish and bake for two hours.

Stewed calf's head and potatoes.—Calf's head, $4d.$; onions, $0\frac{1}{2}d.$; potatoes, one-half stone, $3d.$; total, $7\frac{1}{2}d.$

Wash the head well and leave it to soak for some hours in water and a little salt. Break up the head. Put it, with 1 quart of water and the onions cut fine, into a nice clean pot. Let it boil, and then only keep it at the boil, without boiling, for three hours, and you have a good savory stew to eat with potatoes.

Lentils and rice.—One pound lentils, $1\frac{1}{2}d.$; one-half pound rice, $0\frac{3}{4}.$; onions, $0\frac{1}{4}d.$; dripping, $0\frac{1}{2}d.$; total, $3d.$

Wash the lentils, soak them over night, and put them into a saucepan with 3 quarts of water. Boil for two hours very slowly; then add the rice (after washing it), with onion cut fine and dripping. Let the rice boil until it absorbs all the water. This makes a good substantial dinner.

Rice and cabbage.—One pound rice, 1½d.; 1 cabbage, 1d.; dripping, 0½d.; total, 3d.

Wash the cabbage well and boil it soft in salt and water. Wash the rice and boil it soft and dry. Mash the cabbage well; add it to the rice with the dripping, and pepper and salt to taste. Mix well and serve hot. Good.

Potato pie.—One-fourth pound suet, 1½d.; onions, 0¼d.; one-half pound oatmeal, 0¾d.; one-fourth stone potatoes, 1½d.; 1 pound flour, 1½d.; one-fourth pound lard, 1¼d.; baking powder; total, 6¾d.

Chop the suet very fine, cut the onions small, pare the potatoes very thin, and cut in slices. Take a large pie dish, scatter some suet in first, then some onions, then some meal, and a layer of potatoes, pepper and salt, till all is in. Put potatoes on the top, then cover with a crust made of the flour, lard and 1 teaspoonful of baking powder. Bake for two hours in moderate oven.

Savory meat pie with potatoes.—One-half pound liver, 1½d.; 1 pound scrap meat, 5d.; onion, 0¼d.; 1 pound flour, 1½d.; one-fourth pound lard, 1¼d.; pepper, salt, baking powder; one-fourth stone potatoes, 1½d.; total, 11d.

Cut the meat and liver into nice thin slices. Chop the onion fine. Put a tablespoonful of flour, a teaspoonful of salt, a teaspoonful of pepper on a plate; then mix, and dip your meat and liver in this. Roll a small bit of onion in a piece of liver, then the liver in a slice of meat, and lay it very lightly in a pie dish, heaping it in the center; add water till the dish is three parts full, then cover.

Cover: Flour, lard and a teaspoonful of baking powder, mixed well together, with cold water and a pinch of salt; roll to make nice stiff paste. Cover and bake for two hours. Serve hot with potatoes.

Skirt pie and potatoes.—One and one-fourth pounds beef skirting, 5d.; pepper and salt, 0¼d.; baking powder; 1 pound flour, 1½d.; one-fourth pound lard, 1¼d.; one-fourth stone potatoes, 1½d.; total, 9½d.

Beef skirt is very tender and good if nicely cooked. Cut it across in thin slices. Mix a tablespoonful of flour, a teaspoonful of salt, one-half a teaspoonful of pepper on a plate, and dip each slice of meat in this mixture. Roll up tightly and place in a dish, keeping it well in the center. Fill three parts full and cover.

Cover: Flour, lard, baking powder, pinch of salt, mix well together; add cold water to make stiff paste. Bake two hours. Serve hot with potatoes.

Two dinners from a sheep's pluck.—One sheep's pluck, 6d.; 1 pound onions, 1d.; 2 ounces dripping, 0¾d.; some sweet marjoram, pepper and salt, 0½d.; one-half stone potatoes, 3d.; total, 11¼d.

Split the heart, cut the lights, and soak in water for an hour. Take them out and cut in small pieces. Put a teaspoonful of dripping in a stew-pan with 2 onions cut fine. Let them brown. Add the heart and lights with 2 cups of water, half a teaspoonful of powdered marjoram, let them boil, and keep them simmering for two hours. Serve with potatoes or rice.

Fried liver.—Cut the liver in thin slices. Cut the onions fine. Put a tablespoonful of dripping in a pan; let it get hot. Add the liver and let it cook for about ten minutes, then turn it out on a warm dish. Put in the onions and fry them brown. Mix a teaspoonful of flour and some pepper and salt in half a cup of water, and stir it into the pan with the onions. Let it boil up for a minute, then pour it over the liver.

Two days' dinners for a family.—Ox-foot, 5d.; vegetables (cabbage, turnip, carrot, leek, parsley), 2d.; pot barley, 1d.; potatoes, 3½d.; cheese, 1½d.; flour, 1½d.; total, 1s. 2½d.

First day's dinner, broth, stewed ox-foot and potatoes; second day's dinner, broth, cheese and potato pie.

To make two days' broth, get a good ox-foot, cleaned, wash it well, and put on in 2 gallons of cold water. Boil very slowly for five hours the night before it is wanted, then take it out and skim all the oil carefully off. After breakfast put on the stock that the foot was boiled in (keeping out one pint); add water to make up 2 gallons; wash the barley well and add. Wash the vegetables very carefully, cut them very fine (grating the carrot), and add them, after the barley has boiled slowly for an hour. Keep the lid close on the pot, and boil slowly for another hour, in all two hours. Salt and pepper to taste.

Ox-foot stewed to be taken with potatoes: Cut the foot in nice pieces, put in a saucepan with a pint of stock (if liked, a little of the white part of the leek also). Take 1 ounce of flour, pepper, salt, and a tablespoonful of oil, mix with a little tepid water, make into little balls, and add twenty minutes before you serve on a hot plate, the balls being put round the pieces of foot. Boil half the potatoes, and you will have a good dinner for a large family, taking one-half of the broth, and leaving the other to be warmed up next day and taken with potatoes and cheese pie.

For cheese pie take the other half of your potatoes, pare very thin (as the best part of the potato is next to the skin), and cut in slices. Put in a layer of potatoes, pepper and salt; grate the cheese, put in some, and so on till all is in, then over all put in a large tablespoonful of the oil. For crust take flour and the rest of the oil taken from the foot, and mix with tepid water, a teaspoonful of baking powder, a little salt; roll out and cover pie. Bake for two hours and serve hot.

Soup and haricot of ox-tail.—Good ox-tail, 1s.; vegetables, 1½d.; rice, 0½d.; total, 1s. 2d.

Haricot: Separate the tail at the joints, wipe with a clean cloth. Take the root and divide in four for the first day's dinner, put it in saucepan, and let it get nice and brown; be careful not to let it burn. Then add the half of the vegetables (which should be carrot, turnip and onion), 1 pint of boiling water; let it simmer for four hours. Salt and pepper to taste; serve hot.

Soup: Take the rest of the tail, put on with 3 quarts of cold water, 3 cloves, 1 teaspoonful of mixed sweet herbs, 10 peppercorns, 12 allspice; tie all these in a muslin bag. Let all simmer very gently for three hours. Add the rice, after it has been well washed, and the other half of the vegetables cut very fine or grated, and boil for two hours more with close lid. Serve hot.

Stewed hough.—One pound hough, 5d., cut in slices (by the butcher, to break the bone). Take out the marrow, and put it into the stew-pan with 2 sliced onions and a teaspoonful of flour. Let it brown, then put in the slices of meat, and let them brown for a few minutes; add half a teacupful of water, some pepper and salt. Stew slowly for four hours, with lid very close. Tough pieces of meat can be made very palatable by long, slow stewing.

Take 1 pound of the common dry green peas, having soaked them for sixteen hours in water with a bit of soda the size of a nut; and, after the hough has stewed for three hours and a half, add the peas with a tablespoonful of vinegar, and let them stew together for half an hour. Serve hot.

Stewed steak.—Get 1 pound stewing steak and a piece of suet, which is always given. Chop the suet fine and fry. Dredge the steak with flour and fry very lightly in stewing-pan on both sides. Then add a teacupful of water, boil, then simmer very gently for one hour and a half. Add salt to taste and half a teaspoonful of pepper. A tablespoonful of flour mix in water, add, boil, and serve hot.

This is very good and goes a great way further if you add some vegetables. You can vary the flavor with carrots, onions, parsley, turnips and sweet herbs.

Collops.—Put a little dripping into a saucepan, let it get quite hot, then put in your minced-meat, and keep turning it for ten minutes or so with a fork (if liked, when the dripping is hot, before putting in the meat, add an onion chopped fine and a teaspoonful of flour). When all is a nice brown, add as much boiling water as will cover the meat; close the lid and stew very gently for one hour. Pepper and salt to taste.

Stewed rabbit.—Cut the rabbit into eight pieces and fry till brown, add a teaspoonful of curry powder, quarter teaspoonful pepper, half a teaspoonful powdered thyme, some carrot and turnip cut in slices, two gills of water. Simmer (with close lid) for one and a half hours. Mix 1 tablespoonful flour with water till smooth, 1 small tablespoonful burnt sugar, 1 of vinegar, a little salt to taste, add this to the stew, and boil all another minute or two. Serve hot.

Curried rabbit.—One rabbit, 2 onions, 1 apple, 1 teaspoonful curry powder, 1 ounce dripping and a little salt. Wash and dry rabbit, cut it up in small pieces, put the dripping in a stew-pan, let it get quite hot; peel and chop up the onions, also the apple, fry them till a pale brown; add the pieces of rabbit, and fry them on all sides; stir in a teaspoonful of curry powder, a pinch of salt, and mix well with the meat. Add a teacupful of water, and stew very gently with lid close for an hour and a half. Serve with dry boiled rice for a border round it.

Rice and cheese with green peas.—One pound rice, $1\frac{1}{2}d.$; three-fourths pound dry green peas, $1\frac{1}{2}d.$; one-fourth pound cheese, $1\frac{1}{2}d.$; vinegar, sugar, pepper and salt, $0\frac{1}{2}d.$; milk, $0\frac{1}{2}d.$; total, $5\frac{1}{2}d.$

Wash the rice and put it on to boil in 2 quarts of water, with a teaspoonful of salt. When soft and all the water taken up stir in the milk with more salt, if required, and pepper to taste. Grate the cheese (old cheese is best), mix it in, but keep a tablespoonful to put on the top of the dish. Warm all up in the pot; then turn out on a pie dish. Put tablespoonful of cheese on the top, and let it brown in the oven or before the fire. Get the common dry green peas, soak them for sixteen hours with a bit of soda the size of a bean in the water. Then boil in salt and water. When soft drain, and add 2 tablespoonfuls of vinegar, 1 teaspoonful of sugar, pepper and salt to taste; shake in the saucepan well. Serve hot.

Indian meal and cheese.—One pound Indian meal, $1d.$; one-fourth pound cheese, $1\frac{1}{2}d.$; dripping, $0\frac{1}{2}d.$; total, $3d.$ Boil the meal for one hour, and let it be very thick. Grate the cheese and add with dripping, pepper, and salt. Serve hot. Good after hard day's work.

Potted head.—Half an ox-head, 1s. 6d. Break up the head, wash and soak it in water for a few hours. Boil slowly for five hours in enough water to cover it. Then take it out, and skim the fat off the pot. When cold, lay the head on a clean board, and take the meat off the bones. Cut the meat into small pieces, and put it back into the pot. Add a tablespoonful of salt, a tablespoonful of Jamaica pepper, a teaspoonful of black pepper, a pinch of cayenne pepper, and boil all for half an hour; then put into basins, and let stand till cold and stiff. This, warmed up, will make good dinners for two or three days, with potatoes.

Black pudding.—One quart of blood and skins, 1d.; one-half pound suet, 3d.; and one-half pound oatmeal, 1d.; one-half pint skimmed milk, 0½d.; 1 teaspoonful of mint and a little salt, 0½d.; total, 6d.

Get the blood free from clot. Mix with the oatmeal. Add suet, salt, a tablespoonful of Jamaica pepper, a teaspoonful of black pepper and a teaspoonful of powdered mint. Warm the milk, add and mix thoroughly; turn the skins inside out, and wash them well in warm water and salt. Then rinse them well in cold water, and fill three parts full with the mixture. Tie the two ends together; put them in hot water and boil slowly for twenty minutes. While they are boiling prick with a pin to let the air escape. For serving, toast before the fire, or fry in pan for ten minutes.

To boil potatoes.—Wash the potatoes clean in cold water, put them in a pot with cold water to cover them, and a tablespoonful of salt; boil from twenty minutes to half an hour. Take a fork and feel if their center is quite tender; if so, drain off all the water, put a clean cloth over the potatoes in the pot, let them stand by the side of the fire with lid on to steam. When quite dry take them out very carefully, peel them without breaking, and put them in a hot dish. If the potatoes are watery, put them in boiling water and keep boiling rapidly till done; dry well, and it will make them quite mealy.

How to boil rice.—Half-pound rice, a pinch of salt, a quart of water and a tablespoonful of dripping.

Put on a quart of water, let it boil (milk is better). Wash the rice well. Throw it into the boiling water with a pinch of salt. Boil for fifteen minutes. The rice must be soft, but each grain separate; drain it in a colander and shake it well. Put the dripping into the pot, then put the rice back, and let it swell slowly near the fire for ten minutes. Serve hot.

How to boil macaroni, and to make macaroni cheese.—Put on a a quart of water; let it boil. Add a little salt, then a half-pound of macaroni. Boil for half an hour; drain it in a colander. If for cheese, put one cup of milk into the pan, one-fourth pound grated cheese, a tablespoonful of dripping, a tablespoonful of flour, one-half teaspoonful of pepper, a little salt. Let it boil. Grease the bottom of a pie dish, put in the macaroni. Pour the milk, cheese, flour, pepper and salt over it, and last, sprinkle a little more grated cheese on the top. Let it brown before the fire or in the oven. Two eggs may be added in place of cheese, and a teaspoonful of sugar.

FISH.

Fresh herring, baked.—Fresh herring, salt, pepper, vinegar and dripping.

Clean the herring well, pack them in a baking dish, sprinkle salt and pepper over them, a little dripping and two teaspoonfuls of vinegar. Bake half an hour. Serve hot. Good cold.

To fry herring.—Clean and dry the herring, put some salt, pepper and oatmeal on a plate; dip each herring well in the mixture; have a frying-pan hot with some dripping in it, put in the herring and fry, turn carefully, and fry the other side. Serve hot.

Another way to fry fresh herring.—Cut off the head, fins, and tail, split them up the back; clean well; take out the backbone, scrape them, salt and pepper inside. Take two herrings, place the insides together flat, dip them in oatmeal, and fry for about eight minutes over a clear fire in a frying-pan.

To boil fresh herring.—Wash, gut, dry, and rub them over with a little salt and vinegar; put them into boiling water with a tablespoonful of vinegar, and simmer for ten minutes. When done take them out of the water immediately. If they are to be kept hot for some time, cover them with a clean cloth.

To boil salt herring.—If very salt, leave them to soak in cold water for some hours. Put them on to boil in cold water, and let it come slowly to the boil. When boiling, draw to the side of the fire, and keep at the boil for ten minutes, and take them from the water the moment they are cooked. If salt fish are allowed to boil it hardens them.

Baked sprats.—Sprats, dripping, parsley, salt, pepper and vinegar.

Clean and wipe the sprats gently; mix a tablespoonful of chopped parsley, a teaspoonful of salt, and a half a teaspoonful of pepper on a plate; dip in each sprat, and put in a baking dish, with a little vinegar and a little dripping on the top, and bake for half an hour. Good hot or cold.

Fish pie.—Cod head, 1d.; one-fourth stone potatoes, 1½d.; 1 pound flour, 1½d.; one-fourth pound lard, 1¼d.; baking powder, 0¼d.; total, 5½d.

Get a large cod head, wash it well, place it in a pie dish, and put the dish into a pot with water; but do not allow any of the water to get into the pie dish. The head is to be cooked by the steam. Let the water boil hard for half an hour, then take out the head and remove all the meat from it; boil and slice one-fourth stone of potatoes, put a layer of potatoes into the pie dish first, then fish, pepper, salt, till all are in, adding only any of the liquid that was in the pie dish, then cover with paste.

Salt codfish cakes.—Two pounds codfish, one-fourth stone potatoes, 1 egg, pepper, flour and dripping.

Soak the fish over night. Put it on to boil. Whenever it boils draw it to the side, and let it steam (salt fish should never be allowed to boil, for it only hardens it). When done take out all the bones; have your potatoes boiled; mash them and the fish together, with pepper and salt to taste. Beat up the egg and add it. Make into thin cakes, flour them, and fry them, with dripping, a light brown. Fresh fish can be done in the same way, and is more nutritious.

Fish cooked in its own juice.—One pound fish.

Have your fish well cleaned, wipe it well, and put it into a jar with a clove or sprig of parsley; cover very close, and set it in a saucepan of boiling water, keeping it boiling for half an hour. Serve on a hot plate, with or without sauce.

Fresh fish.—One pound fish, one-fourth pound dripping.

Put the dripping on the fire in a pan to get hot; have the fish cleaned and wiped, cut off fins and tail, sprinkle it lightly with bread crumbs, or flour, or meal; shake off any loose crumbs. Put a crumb of bread into the dripping to see if it is hot enough; if it hisses, it is ready; if it burns, it is overdone. Put in your fish; it will take about ten minutes to fry; have it a nice color. Serve on hot plate. (If you can afford it, you can dip it in egg before you put it in bread crumbs.)

To boil fish.—If the fish is large, with skin whole, it must be placed on the fire in cold water; if it weighs 3 or 4 pounds, it will take thirty minutes to boil. To every quart of water put a teaspoonful of salt, and when the fish begins to boil remove the lid to one side and let it simmer gently till quite done. Have only enough water to cover the fish, or the skin will crack and spoil its appearance.

Steaks or sliced fish.—To every quart of water add a teaspoonful of salt. When the water boils add the fish and allow it from fifteen to twenty minutes for each pound. A tablespoonful of vinegar in the water is an improvement to fish.

PUDDINGS.

Boiled scrap bread pudding.—Any odd pieces of bread. Put into a bowl, pour boiling milk over them; let them stand till well soaked, then beat up with a fork; add a small piece of dripping, a few currants or raisins, a little moist sugar; mix well up, put into a greased bowl, tie a floured cloth over the top, and boil for an hour. Good either hot or cold.

Plum pudding for the million.—One-half pound chopped suet, one-half pound flour, one-half pound bread crumbs, 1 pound grated carrots, 1 pound potatoes, 1 pound currants, 1 pound raisins, 1 pound apples, 1 teaspoonful of ginger, 1 teaspoonful of cinnamon, 1 teaspoonful of allspice, 1 teaspoonful of baking powder, half a nutmeg (grated), 1 pound sugar, a good pinch of salt.

Mix the flour, bread crumbs, suet, carrots, potatoes, ginger, cinnamon, allspice, nutmeg, baking powder, salt, and sugar well; then add currants, raisins (stoned and cleaned), and apples. Mix with water or milk into a soft paste, boil in floured cloth for four hours, or in a basin or mold for five hours. Good.

Brown suet pudding.—One pound flour, one-fourth pound suet, one-half pound treacle, one-half pound raisins, salt, half nutmeg (grated), 1 teaspoonful cinnamon, 1 teaspoonful soda, 1 teaspoonful cream of tartar, milk.

Warm the treacle, chop the suet very fine, mix the flour with a pinch of salt, soda, cream of tartar, nutmeg, cinnamon, all well together; add treacle, suet, raisins, and put in a well-floured cloth and boil quickly for three hours.

Fig pudding.—One pound figs, one-half pound flour, one-half pounds bread crumbs, one-fourth pound suet, 2 ounces sugar, half a teaspoonful nutmeg, 1 teaspoonful cinnamon, 1 small teaspoonful baking powder, milk or water.

Chop the suet and figs fine; mix flour, bread crumbs, sugar, cinnamon, nutmeg, and baking powder well together; add suet and figs, with enough milk or water to make into dough. Roll it into a floured cloth, leaving room for it to swell, and boil very fast for three hours.

Indian pudding.—One quart milk, one-half pound Indian meal, 1 small cup treacle, 1 tablespoonful dripping, 1 teaspoonful ginger, 1 egg, 1 teaspooonful baking powder, a pinch of salt.

When the milk is nearly boiling wet the meal with some of the cold milk and let it boil; then add the treacle, dripping, ginger, pinch of salt, and egg well beaten; lastly, the baking powder. Turn it into a pie dish and bake for two hours.

Cottage pudding.—One cup milk, 1 teaspoonful (large) butter, 1 teaspoonful sugar, three-fourths pound flour, 1 teaspoonful soda, 1 teaspoonful cream of tartar, yolks of two eggs.

Mix sugar, yolks of eggs and butter to a cream; then add the milk and flour by degrees; beat very light, then add soda and cream of tartar, and bake for one hour.

Sauce.—Half a cup of milk, stir in two tablespoonfuls of sugar, beat the whites of two eggs to a slight froth, and stir in; flavor with vanilla before serving.

Swiss pudding.—One pound apples, 2 tablespoonfuls stale bread crumbs, 1 egg, 3 ounces sugar, 2 teaspoonfuls butter, or dripping.

Peel, core, and slice the apples and stew in a covered jar; when done add the sugar and a teaspoonful of butter; when cool, stir in the egg, well beaten; butter the pie dish; strew bread crumbs about an inch thick at the bottom, and as many up the sides as will remain on; pour in your apples, and strew over them the remaining crumbs, and bake for one hour.

Rhubarb or apple dumpling.—One pound flour, one-fourth pound suet, 2 pounds apples or rhubarb, 6 ounces sugar, 1 teaspoonful baking powder, one-fourth teaspoonful salt; if apples, two cloves; if rhubarb, half the skin of a lemon, or a little ginger.

Chop the suet fine, and mix it with the flour, salt and baking powder; then add a little water till you have a nice, stiff paste. Roll out enough of the paste to line your dish, both bottom and sides. Peel and core the apples, cut them into six slices. If it is a rhubarb dumpling, cut the rhubarb in 1-inch lengths, and put it into the basin with the sugar and flavoring. Then take the remainder of your paste and roll it out the size of the top of the basin, wet the edge of the paste lining and lay on your paste cover so that it will stick to it; then flour your cloth and tie it up. Have the water boiling; boil your dumpling for three hours, and turn it out.

A good tapioca pudding.—Soak 3 tablespoonfuls of tapioca in some ginger wine for one hour; then add a little sugar, 1 beaten egg, and some milk. Grease a dish, pour it in, and bake for one hour.

Sago can be made in this way, also bread and butter pudding; using more wine, with a little water and no milk, is a nice change.

Simple trifle.—Six sponge cakes, 2 eggs, 1½ tablespoonfuls jam, 1½ breakfast-cupfuls milk, 1 teaspoonful sugar.

Cut sponge cakes in slices and arrange neatly in a pudding dish; pour a little milk over them, just enough to make them soft, then spread the jam over. Take the eggs and separate the whites from the yolks; lay aside the whites; beat up the yolks in a bowl. Put sugar and a breakfast-cupful of milk into a small pan and bring it to the boil; then pour this over yolks, stirring all the time with a fork; return it to the pan, and stir over the fire till it thickens a little (it must not boil, or the eggs will curdle), then put spoonfuls lightly over the sponge cakes. Whisk up the whites with a knife into a stiff broth, and lay lightly on the top. Stale sponge cakes are very good for this pudding, and are to be had cheaper on Saturday night.

Marmalade pudding.—One breakfast-cupful of flour, 1 breakfast-cupful bread crumbs, 2 ounces suet, 1 teaspoonful baking soda, 1 tablespoonful of sugar, 3 tablespoonfuls marmalade, butter and milk.

Chop suet fine, and put in a basin, add bread crumbs, flour, sugar, soda, and marmalade; mix with a little buttermilk till the whole is wet (it should not be very moist), and beat up a little with a fork; grease a bowl, put in the pudding, and cover with a greased paper; put the bowl into a pot with an inch of boiling water in it, put the lid of the pot closely on and steam for two and a half hours.

This pudding can also be made with syrup, instead of marmalade.

Christmas pies (simple).—One half pound apples, one-fourth pound figs, one-fourth pound currants, one-fourth pound raisins, one-fourth pound sugar, one-half ounce cinnamon, one-half ounce ginger, 1 pound flour, one-fourth pound lard, 1 teaspoonful baking powder.

Peel and core the apples, and cut them into small dice, put them in a basin with the sugar; mince the figs fine; stone and mince the raisins (or use sultana raisins); pick and rub the currants very carefully with a cloth; put all into a basin with the apples and sugar, add the cinnamon and ginger (and any other flavoring that is liked). Mix all well together (the mince is all the better of being prepared some time before it is wanted).

For the crust, mix the flour, lard, a teaspoonful of baking powder, and a pinch of salt, well together, then add enough cold water to make a stiff paste; roll out to about a quarter of an inch thick. The pies can either be made in small tins or soup plates. Rub the tins or plates well with lard, cut the pastes to the right size, put the mince meat in carefully, wet round the edges, and cover the top with paste, and bake in a not too quick oven.

Jam roly.—One breakfast-cup of flour, 1 breakfast-cup of bread crumbs, 2 ounces suet, 1 pound jam, 1 tablespoonful of sugar, a small teaspoonful of baking soda.

Put in a basin the flour, bread crumbs, suet chopped very fine, soda and sugar, and mix with cold water into stiff paste, and roll out into a thin sheet about one-fourth inch thick; take a bowl and grease it with dripping, line it with some of the paste, spread at the foot of the bowl some jam; then lay in a layer of paste, repeating layers of jam and paste, till the bowl is filled; wet the edges of the last layer of paste, and turn down over it the lining of the bowl; cover the top with a greased paper, and put the bowl into a pot with half an inch of boiling water in it; put the lid of the pot close on, and steam for two hours, then turn out.

This pudding is very good made with apples instead of jam.

A few hints on pudding making.—When a pudding is to be boiled, see that the cloth to be used is very clean, and that it is dipped in boiling water, dredged with flour, and shaken well before the pudding is put into it.

If a bread pudding, it must be tied loose. If a batter one, it must be tied tight.

When a shape or basin is to be used they must be well greased before the pudding is put in. When it is ready care must be taken in lifting it out. Allow it to stand for a few minutes before unloosing the cloth.

All puddings must be boiled in plenty of water, turned frequently, kept closely covered, and never allowed to go off the boil.

If the pudding is to be baked, the dish or pan must be also greased before it is put in. Bread and custard puddings require time and a moderate oven to raise them.

As a rule, steamed puddings are put in an earthenware dish, covered with a tight cover or greased paper, which is placed in a pan of boiling water, which must not come more than three parts up the sides of the pudding dish. If the water boils away, more boiling water must be added, and it must be kept always boiling. Be careful in removing the lid that no drops fall on the pudding.

Puddings, etc., when steamed, do not require so much liquid in them as when baked. The dry air of the oven dries them, steaming keeps them moist.

Plain bread pudding.—Any odd pieces of crust or crumbs of bread will make a nice pudding. To every quart allow half a teaspoonful of salt, 1 teaspoonful of grated nutmeg, 3 ounces of sugar, half a pound of currants, and half an ounce of butter.

Break the bread into small pieces, and pour as much boiling water over it as will soak it well. Let this stand till the water is cool; then press it out, and mash the bread with a fork until it is quite free from lumps. Measure this pulp, and to every quart stir in salt, nutmeg, sugar, and currants, in the above proportions; mix all well together, and put into a well-buttered pie dish. Smooth the surface with the back of a spoon, and place the butter in small pieces over the top; bake in a moderate oven for one and a half hours, and serve very hot. Boiling milk substituted for boiling water would very much improve the pudding.

Oatmeal pudding.—One-fourth pound suet chopped fine, one-half pound oatmeal; 2 onions chopped fine, a teaspoonful salt, and half a teaspoonful pepper; mix well together without water; tie it rather loosely into a floured cloth, and boil for three hours.

A cheap dish, and eaten with bread or potatoes. Good and nourishing.

Suet crust for pies or puddings.—To every pound of flour allow one-fourth pound beef suet, half a pint of water, half a teaspoonful of salt, and a teaspoonful of baking powder.

Free the suet from skin, chop it extremely fine, and rub it well into the flour, with salt and baking powder; add the water, and work the whole into a smooth paste, roll it out, and it is ready for use. .

The above, with the addition of treacle or fruit, and rolled up as a roly-poly in a flour cloth, and boiled for three hours, is very good.

Apple sauce.—One pound of apples, peeled, cored, and cut in thin slices. Stew with 1 ounce sugar, half a teacupful of water. Stew till in a pulp, and serve with roast pork, etc.

Mint sauce.—Chop a good handful of green mint up fine, put into bowl with a large tablespoonful of brown sugar, half a teaspoonful of salt, a quarter teaspoonful of pepper and a teacupful of vinegar. Serve with cold meat or lamb.

Brown sauce.—One ounce butter, $1\frac{1}{2}$ ounces flour, half a teaspoonful of salt, a quarter teaspoonful of pepper, a tablespoonful of vinegar and a small onion.

Put the flour before the fire till it is a pale brown, put the butter and onion, cut fine, into the pan, let it get pale brown; add the flour made smooth in a cup of water, a little pepper, salt, vinegar, and another one-half cupful of water; boil and drain.

White sauce.—One ounce butter, 1½ ounces flour, half a teaspoonful of salt, a quarter teaspoonful pepper. Mix together in a pan, add the milk gradually (about two teacupfuls), let it boil, and serve for fish or vegetables. For mutton sauce add to the above a handful of parsley, washed well and chopped very fine.

Pudding sauce.—Two teacupfuls of milk, half a cup of sugar, 2 eggs, a tablespoonful of vanilla. Beat eggs to a froth with sugar. Boil milk and sugar, pour over them, stirring all the time, add vanilla.

Plain pudding sauce.—One tablespoonful corn flour, large tablespoonful sugar, teacupful milk and 1 egg. Beat egg, sugar, and corn flour, with tablespoonful of milk, very light, boil the rest of the milk, pour it over the mixture, stirring all the time.

Preserved rhubarb.—Wipe the stalks of young rhubarb, cut in neat pieces. To every pound of rhubarb add 1 pound of sugar and the grated rind and juice of 1 lemon. Put sugar and lemon on the fire to melt; when melted add rhubarb. Boil for half an hour, taking care not to break the rhubarb. Take it out carefully, put it in jars, let it cool, then cover with paper, and put away for winter use.

To preserve rhubarb for winter use.—Rub the rhubarb well with a damp cloth to take off any sand, dust, or smoke; when perfectly clean cut it into nice pieces about an inch long, and put them into a deep earthware dish. To every 6 pounds of rhubarb add 6 pounds of sugar and one-fourth pound of best whole ginger. Cover the dish and let stand for two days. Then run off the syrup into a preserving pan and boil it for half an hour; then add the rhubarb and boil until it is clear; when it is transparent it is done. Stir it as little as possible, so as not to break the rhubarb (it looks best whole). This preserve will keep for a year.

Apple jelly.—Two pounds apples, 2 pounds rhubarb, 2 lemons, and sugar.

Wipe clean and quarter the apples, remove any decayed pieces, keep in the seeds. Wipe the rhubarb clean, and cut it up into small pieces; wipe and peel the lemons very thin; put all in jelly pan, and just cover with water, add the juice of the lemon, and boil to a mash. Then pour into a jelly bag, and let it drain; measure the juice, and to every pint add 1 pound of sugar. Put the jelly pan on the fire, and bring to the boil, stirring until all the sugar is melted. Let it boil for twenty-five minutes, then skim and pot.

Lemonade with citric acid.—One pound sugar, 1 pint of water, 1 ounce citric acid, 2 teaspoonfuls essence of lemon.

Put sugar and cold water in saucepan and boil. Let it cool; then add the other ingredients, and bottle. A tablespoonful to a tumbler of water.

Sherbet (a refreshing drink).—One-half pound sugar, one-fourth pound tartaric acid, one-fourth pound carbonate soda, sixty drops essence of lemon.

Mix sugar and essence of lemon, and dry thoroughly. Then pass all through a sieve. Bottle and cork tight. For a tumbler of water use a teaspoonful of the mixture.

Boston cream.—One pound brown sugar, 2d. worth essence lemon, 2 ounces tartaric acid, the white of 1 egg.

Put the sugar into 3 quarts of cold water, boil it, pour into a basin, and let it cool. Add the essence of lemon, tartaric acid, and the white of the egg well beaten up. Bottle. One tablespoonful of this syrup to a tumbler of cold water.

Ginger wine.—One-fourth ounce essence of cayenne, one-fourth ounce essence of ginger, one-half ounce tartaric acid, 1 lemon, 1d. worth burnt sugar, 3 pounds sugar, 3 quarts of water.

Put 3 quarts of cold water into a preserving pan, with the rinds and juices of lemon, the tartaric acid and the sugar. When melted take any scum off; let it boil. When cold add the essence of cayenne and of ginger, and add sufficient burnt sugar to give the color you wish. Bottle tight, and it will keep good for three months.

Raspberry wine.—One-half ounce essence of raspberry, one-fourth ounce essence of cayenne, one-half ounce tartaric acid, 1d. worth cochineal, 2 lemons, 4 pounds sugar and 3 quarts water.

Put on the water with the juice and rinds of lemons, sugar, and tartaric acid; let it boil; take off all the scum. When cold, add the essences, and a few drops of cochineal to give the desired color. Bottle tight.

Apple and tapioca tart.—One pound apples, one-fourth pound tapioca, one-fourth pound sugar, 3 cloves.

Soak the tapioca all night in cold water. Peel, core and slice the apples. Put a layer of apples in a pudding dish, then one of tapioca. Sprinkle in some sugar and cloves, and continue this process till all is in.

Cover: Three-fourths pound flour, 2 ounces lard, 1 teaspoonful baking powder. Mix flour, lard, and baking powder, with a pinch of salt, well together; then add water to make a stiff paste, roll out, cover, and bake for an hour and a half.

In the spring rhubarb is very cheap and wholesome, and may be used instead of apples.

Suet can be substituted for lard or dripping, and made into a roly-poly, and boiled for two hours.

BREAD, SCONES, AND CAKES.

To make bread.—Seven pounds flour, 2 ounces German yeast, 1 teaspoonful sugar, 1 tablespoonful salt, a little butter, and a little more than a quart of water.

Mode: Take 2 tablespoonfuls of flour, the sugar and yeast, with a cupful of tepid water (the water to be the heat of new milk), set it near the fire to rise for half an hour. Put all the flour but one handful into a basin, mix well with the salt; if the yeast has risen well, you will have light bread. Add the yeast and a quart of tepid water to the flour in basin, knead it with the hand until smooth; then take the butter and rub over the dough. Cover the basin with a cloth, set it near the fire, let it rise for three hours; then divide the dough into loaves, and bake for one and a half hours in a moderate oven. If the oven is too cold, the bread will not rise; if too hot, it will destroy the yeast.

Wheat meal bread.—Ingredients, 2 pounds wheat meal, 2 teaspoonfuls of baking soda, 2 teaspoonfuls cream of tartar, 1 teaspoonful of salt, 1 teaspoonful of sugar, 2 teaspoonfuls dripping, and not quite a quart of buttermilk.

Mode: Mix the wheat meal, the baking soda, cream of tartar, salt, sugar, and dripping well together; then stir in the buttermilk, and mix quickly and thoroughly for not more than ten minutes. Put into a tin and bake in rather a quick oven for one and a half hours. This will make two loaves at least.

Soda bread.—Ingredients, 2 pounds flour, 2 pounds Indian meal, 3 teaspoonfuls baking soda, 3 teaspoonfuls cream of tartar, 1 large teaspoonful of salt, 1 large teaspoonful of sugar, a little more than a quart of buttermilk.

Mode: Mix all the dry ingredients well together, then stir in the buttermilk; mix well and divide it into three or more loaves, and bake in a tin in a rather quick oven; time, one hour. Very wholesome.

Soda scones.—One-fourth stone flour, large teaspoonful baking soda, one teaspoonful cream of tartar, buttermilk, and a small teaspoonful of salt.

Mix the dry ingredients together thoroughly and lightly; add the buttermilk to make the dough, and divide into from four to six pieces. Sprinkle a little flour on the baking board, and roll out the dough with rolling pin to about a quarter of an inch thick. Cut in four and bake on a hot griddle till of a pale brown; then turn and bake the other side the same.

Steamed brown bread.—One pound Indian meal, half a cup of treacle, salt, 1 teaspoonful baking soda, and 1 teaspoonful cream of tartar.

Mode: Mix meal, treacle, a pinch of salt, baking soda, and cream of tartar well together; then add enough buttermilk to make a firm dough; mix quickly, and put into steamer or basin, and steam in fast boiling water for four hours.

Baked brown bread.—One pound wheat meal, 1 pound Indian corn meal, half a cup of treacle, salt, 1 egg, 2 teaspoonfuls of baking soda, 2 teaspoonfuls of cream of tartar, milk or water.

Mode: Mix wheat meal, Indian meal, half teaspoonful salt, baking soda, cream of tartar well together; warm the treacle and add it, with the milk (or water), to the dry ingredients; put in floured tin, and bake five hours in a moderate oven.

Oat cakes.—Mode: Put 1 pound of oatmeal into a basin, a very small pinch of baking soda, and a small teacupful of tepid water; mix well. Spread some dry meal on the baking board, lay the dough on it and knead with knuckles till you have it half the size wanted. Roll out smooth, and finish with rolling-pin; it should be very thin. Cut in three, and rub well with dry meal on both sides; put them on the griddle. The fire must not be too quick; when quite dry (not brown), take them from the griddle, and toast the other side before the fire till crisp. One teaspoonful of melted dripping is thought by some to be an improvement.

Wheaten meal scones.—One pound wheat meal, 1 pound flour, teaspoonful baking soda, teaspoonful cream of tartar, teaspoonful dripping, half teaspoonful salt, and a little buttermilk.

Mode: Mix the meal, flour, baking soda, cream of tartar, dripping, and salt well together; then add the buttermilk to make a light dough; divide, and roll out to the thickness of a quarter an inch, and bake on not too hot a griddle.

Rice scones.—One pound rice, one-fourth pound flour, 1 teaspoonful sugar, and half teaspoonful salt.

Put the rice, sugar, and salt into a saucepan, with 1 quart

water, and let it come to the boil. Then set it to the side of the fire, and let it steam for two hours with the lid close till all the water has been absorbed and the rice has become soft; then sprinkle the flour on the baking board and turn the rice out on it. Let it stand till cool; then divide into six parts, and roll out very thin. Cut each part in three, and bake on not too hot a griddle.

Potato scones.—Potatoes, flour, and salt.

Take any boiled potatoes left from the dinner; bruise them nice and smooth on the table or baking board; add salt to season; then shake some flour over them or work it in, roll out very thin, prick with a fork, and cut in three. Bake on not too hot a griddle.

Scalded scones.—One pound flour, one-half teaspoonful salt.

Mix the flour and salt together, and add boiling water enough to make a good, firm dough; then divide it, and roll out very thin on the baking board sprinkled with flour. Cut in three, and bake on not too hot a griddle.

Indian meal and flour scones.—One pound Indian meal, 1 pound flour, 1 tablespoonful treacle, 1 teaspoonful baking soda, 1 teaspoonful cream of tartar, half a teaspoonful salt, and buttermilk.

Mix all together, and then add enough buttermilk to make a nice, soft dough; divide it, and roll out each piece into about a fourth of an inch thick. Cut in four, and bake on not too hot a griddle.

Barley meal scones.—Two pounds barley meal, three-fourths teaspoonful baking soda, three-fourths teaspoonful cream of tartar, half a teaspoonful salt, and buttermilk.

Mix, and add enough buttermilk to make a nice, soft dough; then sprinkle a little meal on the baking board, and roll out to a fourth of an inch thick. Cut in three, and bake on not too hot a griddle.

Crullers.—One and one-half pounds flour, one-half pound sugar, one-fourth pound butter, 2 eggs, 2 teaspoonfuls baking powder, milk, and lemon.

Mode: Butter and sugar, beat to a cream, add flour and milk alternately till all are in; beat up the eggs very lightly; grate the rind of the lemon into the flour, and add the juice; then put in baking powder, mix well, roll out to a quarter of an inch thick, divide into small rounds, cutting center out of each to form rings. Fry in hot fat a light brown. The quantities given will make eighty-five crullers.

Cocoanut cake.—One-half pound sugar, 1 pound flour, one-fourth pound butter, milk, 1 cocoanut, 2 eggs, and 1 large teaspoonful baking powder.

Mode: Grate cocoanut. Beat butter and sugar to a cream, beat the eggs very light, and by degrees add the milk and flour; then cocoanut and baking powder, and a pinch of salt. Bake in a tin or mold for two hours.

Small cocoanut cakes (good for children).—One cocoanut, 1 egg, half a gill milk, one-fourth pound sugar, one-fourth pound flour, half a teaspoonful of baking powder, and 1 tablespoonful of corn flour.

Mode: Mix corn flour, sugar, baking powder and flour well together; add milk and cocoanut grated, beat up the egg well, and add. Divide the mixture, and work it with your hands into small cones or drops. Bake on buttered paper in a quick oven.

Ginger bread.—One pound flour, one-half pound treacle, one-half pound sugar, one-half pound lard; 3 eggs, a large teaspoonful of ginger, a teaspoonful of cinnamon, half teaspoonful cloves, 2 teaspoonfuls of baking powder, half a nutmeg grated, a little salt, and milk.

Mode: Melt the lard, sugar and treacle in a saucepan. Beat up the eggs well, mix the flour, baking powder, spice, and a pinch of salt well together; add the melted lard, sugar, treacle, and eggs. Use a little milk to make a soft batter, and bake in a moderate oven one and a half hours. Fruit can be added to this cake—raisins, currants, or almonds—which will make it richer.

Rough robin.—One and one-half pounds flour, one-half pound rice flour, one-half pound lard or butter, one-half pound sugar, 1 pound currants, 1 pound sultana raisins, 2 teaspoonfuls baking powder, 1 teaspoonful ground caraways, 1 teaspoonful cinnamon, and a little salt.

Mode: Mix lard, flour, sugar, baking powder, spices, and a pinch of salt well together, and beat well. Then add fruit. Mix with buttermilk to make a stiff batter. Bake for two hours.

Rice cake.—One pound flour, one-half pound rice, one-half pound sugar, one-half pound butter, 4 eggs, 2 teaspoonfuls of baking powder, 1 teaspoonful essence of vanilla, salt and milk.

Mode: Beat butter to a cream, add the yolks of the eggs and the sugar; beat very lightly. Then add the flour (after being well dried before the fire or in the oven), baking powder, pinch of salt, vanilla, and sufficient milk to make a nice, thick batter. Beat up the whites of the eggs to a stiff froth, and add them last. Mix all very lightly, and bake for two hours in a moderate oven.

Seed cake.—One pound flour, one-half pound sugar, one-half pound butter, 3 eggs, 2 spoonfuls caraways, milk, and a teaspoonful baking powder.

Mode: Mix butter to a cream, add yolks of eggs, sugar and flour (well dried), baking powder, seeds, pinch of salt, and milk to make a stiff batter. Beat whites of eggs to a stiff froth, and add them last. Stir very lightly, and bake one and a half hours.

Sultana cake.—One pound flour, one-half pound sugar, one-half pound lard, 3 eggs, 1 pound sultana raisins, the rind of a lemon grated, 1 large teaspoonful baking powder, salt and milk.

Mode: Mix the lard, flour, yolks of eggs, baking powder, pinch of salt, sugar, and raisins well together; and add enough milk to make a stiff batter. Beat the whites of eggs to a stiff froth and add, mix in very lightly, and bake for one and a half hours.

French cake.—One pound flour, three-fourths pound sugar, one-fourth pound butter, 2 eggs, milk, large teaspoonful baking powder, and salt.

Mode: Beat butter and eggs to a cream; add the sugar and flour by degrees, and mix with a little milk to a stiff batter, or soft dough. Add the salt and baking powder last; mix all well, and bake in a moderate oven one and a half hours.

Pancakes.—One pound flour, fourth pound sugar, one egg, a teaspoonful carbonate of soda, a teaspoonful cream of tartar, buttermilk.

Mode: Beat sugar and egg very lightly, mix in by degrees the flour and milk, work well, add soda and cream of tartar last. Take a little dripping in a piece of clean muslin, rub over the griddle; drop batter in spoonfuls. When one side is done turn them.

Pancakes.—Rub 1 pound of flour, 2 ounces dripping, teaspoonful carbonate of soda, teaspoonful cream of tartar, one-fourth pound sugar, all well together. Add buttermilk to make a soft batter. Rub the griddle over with dripping, and put a spoonful on for each pancake. When one side is done turn. Can be flavored with anything that is liked, or currants may be added.

SICK-ROOM COOKERY.

Mustard Poultices.—Dry mustard, cold water.

Mix enough cold water with the mustard to make it into a thick paste; when quite smooth spread it upon a piece of thin old linen, or cotton; sew it round so as to form a bag. Be careful not to make the poultice larger than required; hold it to the fire for a few minutes, so as not to chill your patient; time, from fifteen to thirty minutes; have ready a piece of clean soft cotton, or a piece of clean wadding, and when you take off the mustard poultice, put on the wadding or the cotton.

Bread and milk poultice.—Stale bread, cold milk.

Boil bread with enough milk to make a thick pulp; spread it on a piece of soft cotton, and apply it very hot. This poultice is often applied without a cloth between it and the affected part, but poultices put into a bag are cleaner and easier rewarmed. Bread poultices are cleansing and soothing.

Linseed meal poultices.—Linseed meal, boiling water.

Put sufficient meal to make the poultice the size required into a hot bowl, and pour on boiling water enough to make a soft paste; beat quickly for three minutes, or till it looks oily. Have ready a flannel, or cotton bag, the size required; pour in the paste, sew up the mouth of the bag quickly. Apply the poultice to the affected part as hot as can be borne.

If ordered with mustard, mix a tablespoonful of dry mustard with the meal. Good for inflammation.

Fomentation of camomile flowers.—Two ounces camomile flowers.

Put into a jar with 2 teacupfuls of water, cover jar very close, let it come to the boil, and infuse for fifteen minutes, keeping lid close on jar all the time; strain off the hot liquor, keep it hot, dip pieces of flannel into it, and apply externally to the part affected. Good to allay swelling and inflammation.

Bran poultice.—Make it like porridge, and put it into a bag. Be sure not to make it so soft that any water will trickle down to annoy the patient.

Linseed or flaxseed jelly for a cough.—One pound linseed, 1 large lemon, one-fourth pound raisins, one-half pound sugar.

Boil the linseed in 2 quarts of water, then let it simmer for three hours; strain; return to the pot with raisins and pulp of lemon, and simmer, without boiling, one hour; strain again, add the sugar. Take a teaspoonful (two or three times a day). This is very good.

Gruel.—Two tablespoonfuls of oatmeal, 2 cups of cold water, half teaspoonful sugar, pinch of salt.

Put the oatmeal into a bowl with the cold water, let it stand for fifteen minutes; then with a spoon press all the water from the oatmeal, and pour into the pan, leaving the meal as dry as possible; put the pan on the fire, and stir it till it boils; then simmer for ten minutes, add the sugar, and serve hot.

Some prefer gruel without sugar, and some with milk instead of water, or a little butter and a scrape of nutmeg.

Barley water.—Two tablespoonfuls of barley, 2 quarts of water, 1 tablespoonful of sugar.

Wash the barley well; put the barley and water into a saucepan and bring it to the boil; then boil very slowly for two hours, strain it, add sugar, and let it cool. Barley water is very cooling and nourishing. The barley may afterwards be used for a pudding, or put into soup.

Beef tea.—One-half pound gravy beef, 2 gills water.

Cut the beef very small; put it into a jar, sprinkle a very little salt over it to draw out the juice of the meat quickly, add the water, cover the jar with paper twisted close over it; let it stand for half an hour; place the jar in a pan of boiling water; keep it boiling for half an hour, and you will have good, nutritious beef tea, easily digested by an invalid.

Veal tea.—One pound veal, 1 large cup of water.

Cut the veal up very small, sprinkle a very little salt over it; put it into a jar, add the water, cover closely with paper; let it stand for half an hour; place the jar in a saucepan of boiling water, and let it boil for two hours.

Suet or milk porridge for invalids.—One tablespoonful suet, 2 tablespoonfuls flour, 1 teacup of milk, a little salt.

Mince the suet very fine; mix milk and flour till smooth, then put into a pan; add suet and a pinch of salt; boil very gently for ten minutes, and serve hot. This is very good and nourishing, especially for those who can not take cod liver oil.

Fish for an invalid.—One small fish, a small sprig of parsley, 1 tablespoonful of milk.

Get a nice, fresh white fish; clean it well; put it into a small jelly jar with the milk and parsley well washed, cover very closely with paper, and set it in a saucepan of boiling water at the side of the fire for half an hour. This is a very light way of cooking fish for an invalid. It can be skinned and boned if preferred.

Egg with tea, coffee, cocoa, or milk.—Break the egg into a teacup, beat with a fork till well mixed; pour in the tea, coffee, cocoa, or milk, gradually stirring all the time. This is very nourishing, and good in cases of exhaustion from overwork or strain.

Lemonade.—One lemon, a large cup of boiling water.

Roll the lemon on the table to soften it; pare the rind very thin (for the white part is very bitter), squeeze the juice into a jug, taking care not to let any pips in, as they are too bitter, add the lemon rind and the boiling water, cover the jug; let it stand till cold, strain and use. Very cooling.

For a pleasant drink add a teaspoonful of sugar; but not in cases of sickness.

Breadberry, or toast water.—One slice bread, a large cup of boiling water.

Toast the bread on both sides till quite dry and a nice brown, but not burnt; break it, and put it in a jug, pour the boiling water over it, and cover; let it stand till cold, and strain. Cooling.

Koumiss, or milk wine.—One quart buttermilk, 2 quarts sweet milk, 4 teaspoonfuls sugar.

Mix the buttermilk and sweet milk together, add the sugar, and stir till melted. Let it stand near the kitchen fire for twelve hours covered with a cloth, then bottle. As it is an effervescing drink, the cork must be tied down and the bottles kept on their sides. When the koumiss is opened it should be used.

ROASTING.

To ascertain the length of time required for roasting, weigh the meat, and allow a quarter of an hour to every pound, and one-quarter of an hour over. If, however, the piece of meat is very thick, allow half an hour over. Young and white meat (veal, lamb, pork,) requires twenty minutes to each pound, and twenty minutes over. They are unwholesome when underdone.

Before beginning to roast sweep up the hearth and make up a large fire in a well-polished fireplace an hour before it is wanted, so as to have it bright and glowing. Do not let the fire go down while the meat is roasting; add small pieces of coal or large cinders occasionally so as to keep it up. Hang the meat, by the small end, to the hook of the jack. When there is no jack the meat may be hooked to a skein of twisted worsted, suspended from a hook projected from the mantel shelf. Wind up the jack, or twist the worsted, so as to make it spin slowly. Place the dripping-pan under the joint. If you have a meat screen, see that it is bright (so as to throw back the heat upon the joint), and place it before the fire. Meat should be placed for the first ten minutes as near the fire as possible, without scorching; the great heat hardens the outside, and keeps in the juices. Baste it as soon as the fat melts. Basting prevents the meat from becoming dry and scorched. Then withdraw the meat 18 or 20 inches from the fire, and baste it very frequently while roasting with the dripping produced by the melting of the fat. If the meat is lean it must be basted with dripping melted for the purpose. The meat may be dredged with flour a quarter of an hour before it is quite ready, to make it browner and to thicken the gravy a little. When it is ready and placed on the ashet, sprinkle it with a little salt. Before making sauce of the brown gravy pour away the dripping from the dripping-pan (keep this dripping for other purposes); add a little boiling water to the brown gravy left in the pan; mix well; add a little salt, and pour it round the roast, not over, or it will sodden the meat.

To roast meat in the oven.—Place the meat in a baking tin, in a very hot part of the oven, for five minutes, to harden the outside and keep in the juice. Baste it as soon as the fat melts; then remove it to a cooler part. Place beside it a cup, or basin, of water to keep the air of the oven moist without cooling it. Baste the meat frequently. For the length of time required, see preceding directions.

All ovens in which meat is cooked should be properly ventilated, in order to allow the escape of an injurious vapor produced by meat when cooked in a close oven. Meat roasted in the oven is not considered so digestible as when roasted before the fire.

Roasting in the pot or saucepan.—This way of roasting is especially suitable for small pieces of meat, and is far more economical, because of the small quantity of fuel required. Melt and heat a tablespoonful of dripping in a pot. Brown all sides of the meat in this, so as to harden the outside and keep in the juices. Then draw the pot to the side of the fire and let the meat cook slowly with the lid on, basting it frequently. Time required, same as in previous directions.

FRYING.

To fry a steak.—Having got your steak, which must not be thinner than half an inch, and not thicker than an inch, take the suet, which is always given with the steak, chop it fine; see that your pan is perfectly clean and dry. Place the pan on the fire with the suet; let it remain until the suet is melted and rather hot. Take hold of the steak at one end with a fork, dip it in the pan, and keep it for two minutes; then turn the other side for two or three minutes, according to the heat of the fire; then turn it. It will take about twelve minutes to cook, and requires to be turned on each side three times during the cooking. Take care that the pan is not too hot, or it will burn the gravy, and perhaps the meat, and lose all the nutriment; you must not leave the pan, but carefully watch it all the time. If not turned very often it will be noticed that the gravy will come out on the upper surface of the meat, which in turning over will go into the pan and be lost, instead of remaining in the meat. Always, in lifting, insert the fork in the fat. Serve on hot plates with salt, pepper, and the gravy round it.

To fry a mutton chop.—Get some nice loin chops, cut the same thickness all through. Have your frying-pan very clean; put in a little dripping or lard; let it get rather hot. As soon as it begins to smoke take the chop with a fork by the small end and dip it in the fat for a minute; then turn it and let it fry for three minutes; you can turn it several times, it will take ten minutes to cook a chop an inch thick with a good, clear fire. Add salt and pepper; have a nice hot plate, and lift carefully, always putting the fork in fat. Pour the gravy round it.

To broil a rump steak.—Get your steak three-quarters of an inch thick (if it should be cut rather thicker in one part than another, beat it well with a chopper). Before cooking a steak stir up the fire (say half an hour before you intend to use it); clear away the ashes; stir all the dead cinders from the bottom, and in a few minutes you will have a clear fire fit for the use of the gridiron. Place your gridiron, with the steak, about 5 inches above the fire, and keep constantly turning the steak, to keep the gravy in. Put the fork, not into the lean part, but into the fat to turn it. One pound of steak three-quarters of an inch thick will take about twelve or fifteen minutes to cook with a nice clear fire. Serve hot on a hot plate.

WASTE IN COOKING.

The following table shows how much is wasted in some of the different ways of cooking:

Four pounds of beef, in boiling or stewing, wastes about 1 pound of its substance; but you have it all in the broth or gravy, if you have kept the pot closely covered.

In baking $1\frac{1}{4}$ pounds is almost entirely lost, unless you have plenty of vegetables in the dripping-pan to absorb and preserve it.

In roasting before the fire you lose nearly $1\frac{1}{2}$ pounds. Do not think you save the waste in the shape of dripping. It is poor economy to buy fat at the price of meat merely for the pleasure of frying it out.

GENERAL HINTS.

It is very desirable that all cooked food should be taken hot. When cold food is taken it reduces the temperature of the stomach; and both the nerves and vessels of the stomach are taxed, in order to bring the temperature of the food thus taken up to that of the human body. So in taking hot soup, tea, coffee, or cocoa we prevent this tax upon the internal organs. When people have been overexerted or had a long fast it is better for them to have a little hot soup or a cup of cocoa, and wait for half an hour before they take their dinner; by that time they are rested, the hot soup or cocoa has refreshed and invigorated the stomach as no wine or spirit could have done.

Before beginning to cook be careful to see that you have a clear fire in a clean grate, and that your pots and pans are thoroughly clean. To clean pots, first clean the inside out well with pot-range, then wash them both inside and out with hot water and some washing soda; then take a cloth, with a little soap rubbed on it, dip it in fine ashes, with this rub the inside of the pot till it is quite clean, then wash it with warm water and dry. Do the lid in the same way.

Fish, if at all plentiful, is always cheaper on Thursdays, Fridays, and Saturdays, and can be had at the time the shops close at less than half price, if they have any over. For those who study economy this is worth remembering, as they can thus provide a good, cheap dinner for the next day.

Pieces of dry cheese, which the grocers are glad to get rid of very cheap, do excellently for cooking and grating.

Soap parings in the same way can be got very much cheaper, and are quite as good for boiling down for washing purposes.

HINTS ON WASHING, ETC.

Washing is always best done early in the week, say Tuesday; then you have the week before you to dry, etc. Mend what requires to be mended the day before. Soak your things before washing; if this is done it saves a great deal of trouble and hard rubbing. Boil the soap, and mix a handful of boiled soap to every gallon of hot water, with a little soda or borax (borax is better for the fine things). Into this put the shirts and linen, collars, etc., to soak all night. Bed and table linen can either be soaked in cold water or laid aside till its turn comes. Curtains or window blinds should always be soaked in cold water to draw out the smoke.

Flannels should be well shaken, to free them from dust, and put together by themselves.

Begin your washing as early as possible in the morning. First light your boiler fire and have plenty of hot water. If it is fine, wash your flannels first. Add a little hot water to the soaked things, taking the best things first. Wash them out carefully, removing all stains. Then put them into another tub with warm water and melted soap, and wash them again; and, as they are finished, drop them into a tub of cold water, and let them lie in it for a while.

Fill up the boiler with cold water, put into it a handful of melted soap, 1 teaspoonful of borax to the gallon of water. Wring the clothes out of the cold water, put them in the boiler, put on the lid, and let them boil gently for a quarter of an hour. Then take them out, add more water, soap, and borax, and put in the next quantity. Pour some cold water on the boiled clothes, wash them and rinse them out, then blue them. Put a little water in the tub and tinge it well with blue. Do not allow things to lie in blue water, but just dip each article in separately, and wring them out. When all are finished hang them out to dry.

If possible, bleach your clothes on grass after boiling; but where this can not be done it is yet possible, with care, to keep your linen white and clear.

Laces and muslin should not be rubbed, but squeezed with the hands in melted soap and warm water. Be careful, in boiling them, to tie them up in a handkerchief to prevent their being torn.

In washing flannels (notice particularly), to keep them a good color and to prevent their shrinking, get from the grocer 1 or 2 pounds (according to the size of your washing) of soap parings, which you will get cheap; for 1 pound of soap parings put 3 quarts of water; boil to a jelly, and with this wash your flannels. Be sure you have plenty of water warm, not too hot. Put in a handful of your soap jelly, and mix thoroughly in the water; then take the flannels, one at a time, shake all dust out of them, then sluice the articles up and down well; rub as little as possible, for rubbing knots the little loops of wool together and thickens the flannel; wring them in a machine, if you have one, if not, squeeze them well. Dry in the open air, if weather permits, as quickly as possible.

In washing scarlet or the blue flannel, put one tablespoonful spirits ammonia in the rinsing water.

For other woolen articles, such as children's dresses, shawls, etc., where there are green or other fancy colors, add to your soap jelly one-half gill of spirits of turpentine, and a tablespoonful of spirits of hartshorn; then thoroughly wash as quickly as possibly; rinse in cold water with a little salt in it, and dry quickly. If this is done carefully, the colors will remain quite fresh.

For prints.—Never rub them with soap. Boil the soap as for flannel, add to water, and wash as quickly as possible; then in the rinsing water put a few drops of vitriol, just sufficient to make it taste a little tart; this will fasten all colors except black, but black fades. For black prints better use salt or a little spirits of turpentine in the rinsing water.

To make hot water starch.—Take a clean basin, and mix to 1 large tablespoonful of starch, 1 teaspoonful spirits of turpentine, 1 teaspoonful spirits of ammonia, with only enough cold water to make into a smooth paste; then pour boiling water (it must be boiling) over it, stirring all the time till it is quite transparent.

To make cold water starch.—To a large tablespoonful of starch put half a teaspoonful borax, half a teaspoonful spirits of turpentine, mix with a little cold water to a paste; then add cold water to make the starch to the thickness of cream; stir well, and put in the things; if the things to be starched are dry, you will have to make the starch thinner.

To starch and iron a shirt.—The linen should be rather damp; dip the front, collar, and cuffs of shirt into the starch, squeeze them well out, and roll up tight for some hours; then shake out and pull them quite straight, leaving no creases; rub them over with a piece of soft cloth. Fold the skirt straight down the back. Iron all the unstarched part first, then the cuffs, then the band. To gloss the front place a smooth board, covered with flannel, inside the breast, rub over the front of the shirt with a damp cloth and iron (with the heel of the iron) very nicely till quite dry and glossy.

In ironing be careful always to rub the iron over something of little value first; this will prevent the scorching and smearing of many articles.

To wash clothes with paraffine oil.—To every 8 gallons of cold water put one-fourth pound soap, shred fine, 1½ tablespoonfuls of paraffine oil, into a boiler; put in the clothes, let them come to the boil, keep the lid close on boiler, and steam for half an hour;

take out the clothes, rub any parts not quite clean, and rinse in plenty of cold water.

To wash clothes in paraffine soap.—Cut down one-half pound paraffine soap, and put it into a boiler of water to melt. Rub the clothes well out of the soda water, in which they have previously been soaked, put them into a boiler and let them boil for half an hour, then put them into a tub with plenty of cold water; wash them thoroughly, then rinse in blue water, and dry.

SANITARY HINTS.

(1) Remember that pure air is food, and that polluted air is poison.

(2) Never allow the air to stagnate in your rooms or houses.

(3) Provide for the constant ventilation of your rooms. One of the best ways of doing this is keeping the window a little down from the top..

(4) Keep the vent always open.

(5) Thoroughly air all sleeping apartments, beds, and bed clothes during the day.

(6) Do not use, for drinking or cooking, water which has long lain stagnant in cisterns or vessels.

(7) See that the water cistern is cleaned out regularly, say every month or two.

(8) See that there is no connection between the water cistern and the drain, and that the waste goes to the outside of the house.

(9) Do everything in your power to keep closets and sinks cleanly and sweet.

(10) See that the private drains from closets are ventilated by pipe opening at the roof.

(11) See that the private drains from closet and sinks are properly trapped, in order that the poisonous gases from the sewers may not get into the house.

(12) The neglect of this precaution is a fruitful cause for many of the worst diseases, such as diphtheria, typhoid fever, etc.

(13) When you need to use disinfectants, as after fever, etc., remember that they do not radically cure the evil. The only remedy is the removal of the causes of impure air or water which has produced the evil.

(14) Avoid the use of covered (or "press") beds, the most wholesome being a plain iron bed without any curtains.

(15) In cases of sickness all utensils, etc., should be kept scrupulously clean, and the precautions suggested above as to maintaining a supply of pure air should be observed with redoubled vigilance.

HINTS ON WHAT TO DO BEFORE THE DOCTOR COMES.

Croup.—Croup, or inflammatory sore throat, is caused by exposure to cold, damp air, or sudden change of weather. The signs are hoarseness and noisy breathing. Give the child a teaspoonful of ipecacuanha wine. If vomiting does not soon follow, give half the quantity. Keep the child in bed. Put a brick into the fire until it is quite hot; place a bucket of water at the bedside; put the hot brick into it, which will raise a large quantity of warm vapor, which the child will breathe. Apply a warm poultice to the throat and use warm fomentations. Milk is the best diet. If the above does not relieve, send for medical advice without delay.

A very good and simple remedy for croup is a teaspoonful of powdered alum and 2 teaspoonfuls of sugar; mix with a little water and give it, as quickly as possible, a little at a time, and instant relief will be given.

Diphtheria.—What goes by the popular name of croup is, in a great many instances, really diphtheria, which is a contagious general disease of great danger. The chief characteristic is the formation of a thick, tough, false membrane on the palate, tonsils, and back of the throat, spreading downwards into the windpipe. The signs are great loss of strength (never absent), the formation of the above-named membrane, sometimes high fever, as often no rise in the temperature. Sometimes eruptions in the skin appear. Whenever the above signs can be traced get medical advice without a moment's delay.

Common cold.—In the case of a child, confine the child to one room, or, if at all feverish, to bed. Apply a warm poultice to chest, and give 10 drops of ipecacuanha wine every hour or two till patient perspires and feels a little sick. In the case of a grown-up person, confine to house and keep patient warm. Mix 30 drops antimonial wine, 80 grains of citrate of potash, 3 teaspoonfuls of syrup, or a little sugar, in 4 ounces of water (an ounce is 2 tablespoonfuls). Give an ounce of this every three or four hours. If the cough lingers, a teaspoonful of paregoric, with 20 drops of ipecacuanha wine in a little water, should be given at bedtime.

Useful homely recipe for a cold and cough.—One ounce Spanish juice, 2 ounces honey, one-half pound treacle, 1d. worth laudanum, 1d. worth oil of peppermint, 1 pint of water.

Boil down 1 pint of water, with the Spanish juice, honey, and treacle in it, to a gill; let it get cold, and add laudanum and oil of peppermint. Bottle tight, and shake the bottle before using. Dose for an adult, a tablespoonful night and morning.

Fainting.—At once make patient lie down, with the head quite low. Loosen articles of dress. Let patient have plenty of air, and keep people from crowding round. Apply smelling salts, cautiously, to nose. Sprinkle face with a little cold water smartly. If faint continues long, or feet and hands are cold, apply hot bottles, and when patient can swallow give a teaspoonful of sal volatile in water, or a little spirits in water.

Fits.—This means either apoplexy or epilepsy. Apoplexy is attended with insensibility. The patient falls, generally, but not always, grows purple in the face, and breathes in a snoring manner. There is paralysis of one side, and the mouth is drawn to one side. Place patient in bed, with head raised. If hot, apply cold water to head, and send for doctor.

In epilepsy patient usually gives a scream, becomes deadly pale, falls on his face, becomes convulsed, and then profoundly insensible. While in this state all that need be done is to loosen articles of dress and keep patient quiet and beyond danger of hurting himself until sensibility returns. It is then a case for medical treatment.

Choking.—Choking arises from food, or fluids, or other substances sticking in the throat or passing into the air passages. In bad choking, where the patient suddenly turns dark in the face, etc., no time is to be lost. Open the mouth and push your forefinger in a determined way over the tongue, right back, and try to hook away or push aside the hindrance. If this does not succeed, you may, by pressing the hinder portion of the tongue, bring on vomiting, and so secure relief. A good plan is sometimes tried with children, viz, that of pressing the chest and stomach against something hard, as a table or a chair, then slapping or thumping the back between the shoulder blades. In this way air is driven from the lungs through the windpipe so forcibly as often to expel the obstacle. When the obstruction consists of a coin, as often in the case of children, a good plan is at once to take the child up by the heels and at the same time give it a shake, or slap its back. Fish bones can sometimes be got rid of by swallowing a mouthful of bread. If these remedies fail, medical help should at once be called in.

Suffocation by gases.—Drag the patient as quickly as possible into fresh air; loose clothing; dash cold water on head, face, and upper part of chest. If the breathing has stopped, artificial respiration must be resorted to.

Poisoning.—Send at once for the nearest doctor, telling him all the particulars, so that he may bring what is necessary. Unless the poison is an irritant, such as oil of vitriol or the like, which burns or destroys the stomach, etc., do all you can to make the patient sick. You may give a tablespoonful of mustard in a tumbler of warm water, or the same amount of common salt with warm water. If the patient is drowsy, as from poisoning by narcotics, you must do all you can to keep him awake by dashing cold water on his head and face, walking him about, etc. Do not permit him to sleep. In cases of poisoning by irritants, emetics should not be given, but you should try to save the stomach as much as possible by giving soothing drinks, as milk, etc. Always try to find out what the poison taken has been. You will generally be able to recognize a case of irritant poison, even if the patient can not tell you, by the stains on the clothes, lips, etc., the burning sensation of the mouth, the terrible suffering of the stomach, the retching, and vomiting of blood, etc. Medical advice must in any case of poison be called in with the utmost haste.

Poisoning by alcohol, or drunkenness.—Get the patient under cover as soon as possible. If insensible, rouse him by dashing cold water on the face. Endeavor to make the patient vomit. Rub the surface of the body with warm, dry cloths; wrap the patient in blankets; put hot water bottles to his feet, and do all you can to keep up the heat of body, which is always lowered in the state of intoxication.

Broken limbs.—The thing to be first done is to keep the limb quite steady till the surgeon comes. This is done by placing on each side of the broken limb whatever may be at hand, such as slips of wood, small pillows, an umbrella, the stock and barrel of a gun, or two walking sticks, or even firmly rolled straw, or pads of cotton wool, and retaining them in their position by one or two handkerchiefs, not tied too tightly. Never raise the patient from the ground until the nature of his injury has been ascertained, or some appliance has been made to prevent the movement of the broken limb. Then raise him, if possible, with the help of several persons, and, as it were, in one solid piece, all moving together, and keeping step in carrying. If a patient has to be carried home, let it be on a shutter, or a table, or a stretcher, on which he can lie flat, instead of being doubled up in a cab, as is often done. It is from neglect of this simple rule that broken bones are often made to protrude through the flesh, simple being thus turned into compound fractures, attended by the risk of the limb being lost.

What to do when dress catches fire.—The following are the directions given in Dr. Robert's book on ambulance work : " If your own dress, throw yourself at once on the ground, so that the rising flames may not catch the upper part of your clothes nor burn your head and chest; roll about (so putting the flames out by pressure), and at the same, if possible, wrap yourself up closely in a rug, hearth rug, blanket, table cloth, overcoat, or carpet, so as to smother the fire. Do not get up to call for assistance, but for that purpose crawl to the bell rope or door. If another person's dress, throw the person on fire down at once, wrap him or her up in a rug or something similar, or, if there is nothing at hand suitable, use your own coat, rolling the patient about in it, for the purpose of smothering the flames." A woman rendering help in this way must exercise great self-possession, and be careful not to get her own clothes entangled in the flames.

Measles and scarlet fever.—When measles or infectious diseases are prevalent in a neighborhood, and a child shows symptoms of cold in the head and fever, it is a reason for immediate carefulness. The diet should be light, cooling, scanty, and the child should be kept indoors. In its ordinary course measles is unaccompanied by danger, but the mildest form may be quickly converted, by want of care, into the most dangerous. The parent should carefully watch the symptoms of change, and if a child complains of piercing headache, intolerance of light, etc., the doctor should be called in at once. It is also most dangerous to resort, without advice, to spirits and such remedies to bring out the rash if it suddenly disappears. Sometimes the disappearance of the rash may be traced to careless exposure to cold. In this case the child should be instantly, and without hesitation, put into a warm bath, care being taken to prevent subsequent cold. Often, however, the cause of the disappearance may be dependent on internal inflammation or too high fever, and medical advice should be at once procured.

Indigestion.—Among the most common causes of indigestion are the undue use of strong or too long infused tea (which, taken without food and in excess, is destructive), the use of new bread, and eating too fast.

Teeth.—If people wish to preserve their teeth they should brush them, especially at night, gently with a short, soft brush, moved up and down so as to remove remnants of food, etc., lodging between the teeth, and so destroying the enamel. This precaution involves little or no expense, and the trouble will be well repaid. When iron tonic or acid mixtures have to be taken they should always be sucked through a glass tube, which can be got at any chemist's for a penny or two. Doctors often forget to remind patients of this, and, in consequence, the teeth grow prematurely black or loosen and decay.

Recovery from sickness.—When patients are recovering from measles and scarlet fever the greatest care must be taken to avoid chills. From the neglect of this precaution after-consequences of the most serious character often occur. Children recovering from these illnesses should be warmly clothed and kept out of cold draughts until they have quite regained strength. It is also the duty of parents who have children suffering from the above diseases to prevent healthy people from coming near them, particularly in the case of scarlet fever, until the stage of peeling of the skin is quite over, when the patient should be well washed with carbolic soap. The bed and bedding should be disinfected as well as the clothing.

Intoxicating drink.—The abuse of intoxicating drink is the curse of this country. It is the fruitful parent of crime, disease, premature death, and domestic misery in every shape and degree. The judges, with one accord, say that if the people could only be made to abstain from the use of intoxicating drinks more than half the prisons might be shut up. Men and women who are tempted to sin in this way should abstain entirely. For these there is but one rule of safety—taste not, touch not. Industry, thrift, and strict temperance, these are the simple rules which, by the divine blessing, secure health and lasting happiness.